GW00399957

KIM TAPLIN

BY
THE HARBOUR WALL

ENITHARMON PRESS

First published in 1990
by the Enitharmon Press
40 Rushes Road
Petersfield
Hampshire GU32 3BW

ISBN 1 870612 75 2

Set by Bryan Williamson, Darwen
and printed by
Antony Rowe Limited, Chippenham, Wiltshire

ACKNOWLEDGEMENTS

Acknowledgements and thanks are due to the editors of the following magazines and anthologies in which some of these poems first appeared: *Celebration, Challenge, Country Life, Home Truths, Oxford Poetry, Peace News, Second Nature, Writing Women.*

The *Muniments* sequence has been published as a pamphlet by Jackson's Arm, and four of the poems in it have been set to music by Robert Sherlaw-Johnson in fulfilment of a commission by the Welsh Arts Council.

| |

For Nat

CONTENTS

I

LAPWINGS, FOR INSTANCE

It pleases me to see the plovers come back,
small flocks of them flickering high in the blue,
catching September sunlight as they move,
round wings lapping the air as a cat laps milk;
to hear them crying *pee-oo-wit!* over the turned earth...

And because the idea of God can become all but a vice,
gripping the mind so that it can't be moved
but can only look forward to eternity,
it's only things like this that still ring true.
History, too, hinders; it can be a halter:
the difference is you face the other way.
...Though without these we are locked in the quotidian
like beasts...
                    But whereas it was once enough
to sing a few notes of the unending symphony
meaning, *This is the present, This is where I live,*
and that would be prayer
and would acknowledge the humus enriched
with so much blood, now we must add a motif
to show we can move and be moved to refuse
man-made unmaking.
                    Somehow I must set
a patient repetitious *Let it live*
low but insistently like Schubert's quail
in all my celebrations of this now,
and in my crying over the turning earth.

FOR CHRISTINA

Remember the frosty day we went to Tynemouth
and had cheese scones for lunch and pots of tea
and saw a plaque that said 'Here Harriet
Martineau stayed and regained her health'
and couldn't remember what else Harriet did
but being women out for a fine February
walk who hoped the sea air might do us some good
were glad to hear it anyhow?

We all talked nineteen to the dozen
were frank and friendly in sisterly fashion –
there was your friend Mary and her friend Di –
though I expect I showed off –
I don't remember. I know I paddled
and it made my feet ache.

But what I couldn't say then and now
I'd like to is about the birds on the rocks
at Cullercoats, how I saw them there
as *native and endued* and us as not
having a proper habitat – *strangers and pilgrims* –
and it made me home-sick. But also that

the lie of the land brought waves in long curved lines
and their sound was soothing and continuous
less than a roar but loud enough when I let it
flood in to rinse and scour the trivial negative
thoughts that infest my mind and feel much better,
and this is something that I owe to you
from the day we went to Cullercoats and Tynemouth.

GIFT

Dullard at concerts,
gaping at beauty that's beyond me,
sometimes a trumpet's peal
stirs muddy understanding like a silver eel.
But still I passed an ear for music on,
go-between with a gift for someone else.

Once when you were a baby we
for some reason wandered round a church
and unexpectedly the organ played:
you became rapt.
I was half-glad and half-alarmed,
as though you'd learned to talk to whales.

Later, after you'd played for the first time
in Second Orchestra at school,
you tried to tell me your delight:
The strings went – here you sang –
then all the woodwind
came in quietly ...
But chiefly from the glow there was on you,
like a low sunset makes late in the day
on a companion's face, you made me see
what we can look like turned the proper way.

MOTHBALLS

Someone walked past me with a whiff of camphor
and I was back by Granny's chest of drawers
trying on feathered hats in the tilted glass...
cupboards of linen laundered flawlessly...
wanting to try my hand at scything nettles,
and cutting so they fell back on my arm...
and, yes! that other smell, of chicken mash,
hot mealy scraps in a huge simmering pan...

I wakened to a sudden sense of loss
for a world where moth corrupted when it could
and only providence could make things last;
and for her friendship that I failed to nurture,
from misplaced loyalty and then from fear.
From now on I'll keep house more carefully.

CLIFF PATH, DYFED

Briefly, before the dazzle took effect,
we saw the far-down sea,
its rough roar muted to a purr,
a quiet nut hatch-blue recalling inland woods:
the whole wild shore appearing tamed by height.
The rocks looked separate and neat like turtle's plates.

Descending by the zig-zag: celandines,
toothwort and one round crust
of fiery lichen on a post.

Now we are down we clank across the stones
and bare our feet at last
on hard wet sand scoured smooth,
walk gratefully on a reflected sky.
Behind us, stern black cliffs splashed orange;
tumbled rock.

A little ridge of fudge-like sand dissolves
in trickling streams at the first lick
of the incoming tide.
Hushed by the rush of sound we stand
and wait for it to wet our feet.

RAOUL DUFY EXHIBITION:
HAYWARD GALLERY, JANUARY 1984

Eyes shine all
round me, lips part, foreheads ease for the moment from stress –
so many faces reflecting your resonant yes.

Blue above
everything, harvest, brave sails on the titupping sea,
holiday happiness, music of Mozart, such free

generous
gifts in return for the gifts that were given to you.
Never a hint of the pain that was given you too.

Do I feel
doubts about Henley and Ascot and Deauville and Nice?
You saw life's colour and flight, not man's virtue and vice.

Someone who
knows-all about it is showing his friend what he sees:
fit that to do it the expert goes down on his knees...

Journeyman,
painter pursuing the rarer techniques of your art,
study how Raoul unravels the knots round the heart.

WALKING IN NORTH DEVON

All day I slowly creep across the map:
walking strange country I'm
forced into learning how to read the signs.

These high-banked lanes keep the wind out; men trod
them deeper over years,
made safe and secret runs like field-mouse lines.

The roads are wet still after last night's rain.
A tiny yellow snail
starts travelling across the shining tar:

five freckled toads lie flattened here – how come?
I turn one with my stick
puzzled, considering how quick toads are.

Riches of ragwort, and a late hedge rose,
mallows, a foxglove, vetch,
crowd in bedizening one snail's domain.

Wheel within wheel, the rings of hemlock seeds
excite me evilly
to fancy I could munch on them and gain

power: nature at first stirs passions up
like a wasps' nest, that one
by one fly off and leave me, quieter, here.

And as the road climbs up past pink-washed farms
to high and lonely moor,
thick cloths of cloud slide off to show the clear

chicory blue of an unguarded sky.
Lightened at last, I call
silently, *Ah, Lord Proteus, is it you?*

True, echoes emptily until I shift
my grasp and lose him: rain
begins to fall, lightly at first, and now

blotting the landscape, forcing down my face,
falls heavily and cold.
I set my teeth and grimly hold my pace.

II

March

Grey sky. A grey heron by grey water, waiting.

Hail, rain and wind begin the spring,
bruise the hyacinths, scour the sky to a clean blue
and break some of the Lent lilies,
small pale daffodils that ease the way to Easter.

The river runs back up its old dry leats
and next morning the meadow is under water.

Between storms cloudscapes in the Whitehill hollow,
great-bellied mounds of dark and white cumulus,
bare trees become shining song-posts for blackbirds.
Ripples glint, celandines gleam,
"down at th'Arches" the river reflects
and a swan with arched wings is a cloud among clouds.
A little, chill wind stirs its feathers
and wafts the cries of lambs and mothers
mingled over the hill.
Palm Sunday. Nat saw jack hares boxing.

The elms by Akeman Street have seen their last
spring. No early flowers, the earth receives
no scattering of seeds as in the past.
The saw-edged crispness of those tiny leaves,
home-thoughts kept green in mind, will not
this year or ever more break from the dry
twigs, giving cool harbour for sheep on hot
summer days and shelter from stormy sky.
A rook or two, unable to adapt
or loyal despite misgivings, makes again
a messy nursery; and having tapped
shells and fed full they'll fledge: trees wait in vain.
Black blunderers, they cannot understand
loss no hoarse hankering can countermand.

21

Puddles in the lane are the colour of old pennies;
but the laneside ditches are covered in virid slime,
and fool's parsley, small new nettles
and furled lords-and-ladies with hidden phalluses
green the drab banks.
                        A pair of pigeons
flap out of the may-tree like shaken pillows,
the wind in the ivy sounds like scrubbing,
and the washed pasture springs with fresh brown molehills.

April

Birds singing, buds breaking, broken eggshells.
A fledgeling perches on the open window.
Blackbirds open daffodil beaks, more jubilant than ever,
though a brown hen-bird hunched in the hedge
hatching a third clutch for the carking crow
could give them the lie in the throat,
or the north wind blowing wintrily for days on end.

But blue-tits tumbling in the pussy-willow
look catkin-soft and pollen-yellow
and brimstone butterflies are airborne primroses.
In Peter's Spout kingcups come out like suns
bright swallows swoop for gnats above the stream
old willow trees are putting on new leaves
and willow-warblers tinkle all day long.
Bees hum and plunder the white plum-blossom.
Sweet-scented violets with heart-shaped leaves
dark or pale purple, pinky-brown or white,
make even dreary bits of scrub look lovely.
And always, one day, listen! There's the cuckoo –
as queer and seasonal as mistletoe.

And if the thrush seems to say "be good, be good"
from a hidden pulpit in the garden,
it is because it's easy to be grateful
after a day of delicate beauty, when the dusk
softens soft green still more and shows the hill's
long smooth slow curve against the light behind,
and the children chase a half-seen shuttlecock.

May

Deep greenness, damp and misty after thunder,
mist of parsley in the lanes
mist of bluebells on the Heath.
The lanky cuckoo calls continually.
The birthday of our first child, Phoebe May.

Dawn frost gives way to warmth and by midday
William the cat lies panting on the path.
Oli stakes up each one of my sweet peas
with little individual bits of string
and Zo is raking piles of grass together.
Everyone's arms and necks smell pleasantly.
A jug of apple-blossom scents the stairs;
a swarming bunch of bees hangs on the tree.
The beards of barley are just tinged with purple.
On golden evenings rabbits graze green wheat
until the dark shuts up the dandelions
and dew falls on their fur.

The blossom on the old black plum
gleams softly, and gives faint sweet scents.
Daisies are shut among damp bents
and clover. *Look, the moon has come,*

still soft and hazed as though from bed.
And suddenly the evening star
shines, properly crepuscular,
waking before the light has ebbed.

A half a dozen blackbirds still
sing rich arpeggios or lark,
scaring each other in the dark
as summer-wakeful children will.

Here in the Cotswolds they were haymaking,
and the poor stuff that passes for hay now
had still a summer smell;
while in the South Atlantic English soldiers
made ready for a final mowing
on a winter sea.
It's nearly June before the may is out,
heaped heavy flowers for spring's funeral.

June

As though every thing were not already astir –
bluebottles prinking, larks singing,
dragonflies darting, yellowhammers calling
again and again –
a warm wind bandies the sounds about,
makes a stand of docks nod as though they were speaking,
ruffles running water into rough green diamonds,
opens a pool of blue in a smoky cloud mass
from which the remote mote of a swift
swims like a freed prisoner.

The sward above the ancient spring is singing
with buttercups and daisies. Shell-pink roses
hang over the river underneath an oak
strewn on the shingle sound of its shaken leaves.
The Heath breathes the sweet smell of honeysuckle
and bracken rears, a shoal of seahorses.
June's a warm sea and nature bathes in it.

The seasons do not cease because we fail,
whatever colour the new government is.
Rainfall and starlight are still sweet although
people are rioting in Liverpool,
England is occupied with foreign troops
and Irish Christians daily kill each other.
Nor does domestic anger change the weather.

The Whitehill willows keep an open house
to ivy, hawthorn, roses, redcurrants,
brambles, buckthorn, grass and nettles...
Phoebe and I pick pounds of gooseberries there
and make them into jam.

We all play frisbee in the long damp twilight
and later when we've gone in we hear a chink
that brings us creeping to the open door again
to see the hedgehog snuffling up its milk.

July

Fine morning. We are up first thing and find
three garden tigers guarding the back door.
It is already hot.
                    Later we swim
and bring back yellow lilies for the table.
The Cherwell is alive with damsel-flies.

This is the month of little field-edge flowers,
hop-trefoil, creeping buttercup, heart's ease and clover,
when marshy Peter's Spout smells warm and minty
and meadowsweet is heavy in the air.
Phoebe keeps finding tiny thumbnail frogs.
There are sweet peas for picking every day,
lifting the lassitude of the sultry Dog-star.

Swallows and swifts possess the evening sky.
Across the river Mr Hunter
in a brown overall is stacking bales;
the setting sun is glowing on his face.
We walk the fieldpath to the fair in Tackley,
Indian file through the popping barley.
On the way back our feet brush dew-damp grass.
Was that an early bat or a late swallow
skimming down the lane?
                                   With dark comes rain at last
bringing relief as withheld tears do,
and someone quickly pulling windows shut
unwittingly caught a hawk-moth in the house
where it had followed strands of honeysuckle.
After squalls all night from the south and west
we found next day the bean-row had blown down
and the hawk-moth sitting still inside the glass,
a creature hardly ever seen by day,
with alien candy stripes of pink and green.
It sat all day beside the open window
and in the evening vanished silently.
On the last day of July Nat was born.

August

We put the bean-row up again more firmly,
scarlet flowers against the blue sky
between white fleeces of cloud.

Harvest is half-done. Distant wheat
is pale-ripe in the sunlight, "white already",
but the field behind the house is not yet cut
and seen close to's more brown than gold
with patches of it beaten flat.
Some fields are black after the stubble-burning,
but here and there the aftergrass shows green.
The children found a dead snake full of eggs.

Some mornings ground mist lingers until ten.
Birdsongs are over, but you watch the sky
for signs, the gold edge of a great grey cloud
or rays splayed downwards from a hidden sun.

Christina puts a vase in every room,
with reddish leaves, or flowers from the herb-bed,
when no-one else finds anything to pick.
I move more caterpillars off the kale
and cut some lavender for Christmas bags.

We shake the branches for the early apples.

September

Thick dew. Cobwebs. Leaves turning and starting to fall.

Peewits stand on the plough like a new crop
still, all facing one way.
As though someone had planted dragons' teeth.

On a gold afternoon in late September
a butterfly roosts on the warm wood of the trunk,
discloses dark fur with flame-red ribbons
and piebald patches, against the brown bark;
closes and opens and closes,
and at length lays itself open
basking

27

October

Diana comes home with a bundle of wallflower plants
and together we plant them in between the bulbs.

Red admirals are still flying
or resting still on mauve Michaelmas daisies.
This year's brown robins redden like rose-hips,
and their autumn songs are crisp and sharp as apples.
Fieldfares come as the leaves are leaving,
breaking free and going to ground.

We walk in the brisk wind.
Partridges take to the air like flying clods
and merge with the earth when they come to rest again.
A squirrel busy underneath the beeches
is grey with the grey of the smooth boles
and under the puffed fur of its tail
tawny, and tawny-faced, to match the leaves.
Whatever are these things? Look at these fungi!
Brown eruptions, stalkless, split strangenesses...
At home we looked through *Flowerless Plants*,
uneasy till we'd given them a name,
and found that speech had spanned their paradox:
Earth Stars.

The leaves are swept across the sky
and burn for a few seconds in the sunlight
or else are stirred in circles on the ground
as though someone were making beech leaf soup.
But as the month goes on they come to rest
and the mulch grows darker, richer, underfoot.

November

Cold breath disturbs the upper fog,
reveals and then re-veils a sharp-edged disc
as white as paper and no brighter
like the dead body of the god we eat in church.
The windows rattle.
The wind plays owl in the chimney.
No-one wants to go out
because the old man's beard is dingy and draggled
and the haws are brown and old
and the wind works on the damp sycamore leaves
black-spotted like a sinful soul
twisty twisty, till they drop.
Yet if you go you find white deadnettles
and a late vetch in flower
and a meadow covered with yellow hawkweed
as though it were still summer.

Russet oak leaves rustle
brown ash go *shish shish*
dry hops are the lightest of all like the scitter of mice —
oh, if only I were a steadier scholar, apt
at learning the whole wild orchestra,
ear-skilled and eye-skilled
and not so nesh.
November's dreadful for despair and doubt.

The lawn's in shadow, but the sun makes spears
of winter gold across it through the trees.
The trees are silent; it's the wind one hears
moving the branches and the last few leaves.
The trees are still, it is the wind one sees,
whose dance by their abandonment appears.

December

Now only sodden haulms are left to mark
where peppery lupins and rank golden rod
boldly caught fire and flowered, where sweet beans
lay tender in their sappy, fur-lined pods.
Now days are short and all that seem to grow
are stripped and stinking yellow stalks of sprouts.

Mixed weather at the solstice:
dry grass gold in the sun,
blue sky, rain clouds, a double bow.
Then a red sunset, lighting dark blue tufts.

Soon a very cold night, with white stars,
the Pleiades a well-filled pin-cushion.
Then snow, large-flaked and lying,
blue-shadowed snow,
so white it makes the swans look brown and dirty.
Here green-gold juice of rotting elder leaves
has leached out into it;
there rabbit droppings dot it like sprig-muslin.
The cold continues, affecting the spirits:
in a hard winter there's no getting away from it.
It was bitter in 1981
when we heard just before Christmas
Colin had killed himself.

We went as usual to cut some holly
from the old tree alongside Akeman Street.
Dragging it home in silence in the wind
was work and affirmation, which we needed,
and still do.
Each year his absence and our grief
enters the other, happy festival

shaming us into greater tenderness.
But still it's one gift that we can't accept.
When will our brief, unrooted lives make sense?
this year, next year, sometime, never?

January

Some days are never properly light:
testing weather for resolutions.
Small birds keep coming into the laundry room:
one fear drives out another, as with us.
Once Nat found a dazed and starving pigeon
and brought it in and warmed it for a while.
Being under Pound Hill means sometimes no cars get through;
then we fetch milk and letters with the sledge.
Flock after flock of redwings going south
cry their high calls in a snow-filled sky.
Thousands always leave it too late to move;
you find them vainly tearing frosted greens.

But it can be so soft, if the snow goes,
and you stand at the sheltered corner of a copse,
out of the wind, feeling the *sun*,
by a field of three-inch corn,
scenting a fox, watching the shadows slide,
hearing birds start to sing in the open weather.
Smells, sights and sounds revive the earth and heart
from a long frozen sleep.
Here are the blue-green spears of daffodils.
The heart recovers from its cryogen
and starts to cry: too soon.

February

Cold fog clings to the black branches.
Twig-drops freeze and fall as beads of ice.
Hey, look! It's snowing again. We watch
small icy snowflakes falling in the lamplight:
it gives a pleasant zest to our log fire.
But morning shows the grass has gone again –
and we have had too much of black-and-whiteness.
I try to find some good in the east wind
but I am sick at heart and have catarrh.
When the thaw comes to stay the earth and I
cannot respond at once; it took too long.

Ground had forgotten the forget-me-not
blue of the sky above unyielding fields;
but lane-ruts show the blue they never show
except on puddles made from melted snow.
Snowdrops in the churchyard! Yes, they're beautiful;
only they're still that penitential white...
In snow years I'm more glad of the cock bullfinch's
vulgar baboon's-bum red and black and blue,
although he's vandalising plum-tree buds.

Then, near my window,
so close I see the small steam of his breath,
a striped hedge-sparrow sings of springtime
sweet-so-sweet so sweetly

III

The sea sparkles.
On days like this everything
good seems possible, even likely.

By the harbour wall,
where the eye can see clean
to the bottom and the stones
show themselves in their true colours,
small wooden boats ride gently up and
down, at rest but ready,
shaped like eyes.

I run mine over them,
over and over,
as a hand smoothes the flank of a horse.
The curved planks are
just what is needed.

And I'm seized with longing to live like that,
and especially to write like that –
trim poems built in the age-old ways...

but a salesman thrums with a credit card
and intones with a sneer occupational lies
There's no call, no call, we get no call at all
(with his howl of longing battened under hatches)
Most people go for fibreglass.
Lighter to handle. Low maintenance.
(Oh yes, a poem needs to be maintained,
copied and learned and read aloud for love, but)
Most people go for fibreglass...
Comes cheaper for one thing.

35

And the sparkling sea is fouled
by the flux from our sick bowels.
I'm infected. I'm dying.
Craft? What's the use of trying.

The use is what it always was except
that now as well as individual souls
we have a planet's life to conjure with.

THE DAYLIGHT TERRORS
OF THE EARTHCHILD TELEMACHOS

Hurrying through the hall
I heard a farmer call
"Give the old tart a fix!"
and follow it with kicks.
Never were such brutes as
my lady mother's suitors:
contemptuous of her health
they only want her wealth.
O true and patient wife
I fear for your life.
Lord, leave your odyssey:
bring back true husbandry.

GARDEN BIRDS

The ruthless cat is mine, that preys on birds;
So is the garden, and the guilt, if any.
Mine: yet the cat, impervious to my words,
Goes, as cats will, its way. Sometimes, of many
Quick small ones it takes, one I will preserve,
Holding it tenderly in my huge hand,
Where it lies still, pulsing, but every nerve
Fear-frozen; ears deaf, eyes as blind as sand.
The cat they know and reckon on. Some bold
Spirits even mock at it, but no such jeer
Of recognition greets me. I, alone, am cold.
How can so slight a frame hold so much fear?
Warm, light, most frail, why can you not love me?
The black cat sees me, weeping, set you free.

MONOLOGUE

Oh what a relief it is
to be able to talk to you like this
after years of talking to myself.
There are so many things
I want to ask you.
Why did you never
answer before?
Why didn't you leave
some kind of message
if you couldn't come?
I felt like a girl
at the door of a dance hall
who's been stood up.
And sometimes it was worse:
sometimes I wondered
if I hadn't been terribly
mistaken about you.
I had a horrible dream one night
in which...no I can't say.
You know anyway
you know what you did; I mean
you know what I dreamt.
How long have you known
what I felt about you?
Do you really love me?
Oh God, where are you going?

I
I shall not want

Not want?
When my desire is like a tree
roots reaching down, branches bearing up
ten thousand leaves on the lookout for sunlight,
when my smallest wish is a ravening beast
blind, deaf, only a yawning maw?

Not want,
when longing lies at the centre of my soul
like an unhealing wound,
when every stirring of sweetness only reminds me
of what I have lost
and want?

I want all manner of things
to be well.
I want you and you and you
down to and including the least fly
to be happy.
Not want? And shall I not?

II
Beside the still waters

my burning thirst will be quenched
and my burning anger cooled
and my mind washed clean of its filth.

And everyone that I have failed to love
everyone I know
will come towards me holding out their arms.

The water will be fresh and not salt.
Weeping won't be needed any more.

III
The paths of righteousness

are bordered with tiny flowers
like the ones that grow at the edges of cornfields.
They are wide enough for two or even
three friends to walk abreast
and made of soft turf.
No! I am not a false prophet.
What I say is true.
Only they are very well-hidden:
we have trouble finding them.

IV
I will fear no evil

if the only thing I fear
is causing pain because
although I cannot cease
to cause it while I live
if I keep my eyes on
that, as long as I watch
that, I shan't be able to see the demons of
despair making ugly faces at me.

V
In the presence of mine enemies

I shall find a way of making merry
that will not seem triumphant
and I won't pretend that I don't see their sneers.
I shall see that our pain is the same.
I shall ask them to sit down and really want them to,
and they will feast with me and be my friends.

Love is the smooth oil on my head.

VI
In the house of the Lord

there will be no poisonous pride
no scabby sloth
no slavering fits of anger
no sacrilegious greed
no covered, festering covetousness
no lust
no cancerous envy
nothing
but the space of love

Here all unlikely, incredible journeys end.
We loose each other's shoes
we bathe each other's feet
and then all those who came home first
bring in the supper, smiling.

CHICORY
for Robin Tanner

Whenever I see chicory
which has tall bare woody stalks
and grows on dry roadside verges
it pierces my all too effective armour straightaway
and it happens because its flowers
are that particular blue.

Robin knew it, he called it cerulaean
and I think he was right because
sometimes you lie in the grass,
certain clear days with no cloud
or only scraps to go wool-gathering,
and you want to go up and up and into the sky –
Jefferies called it 'the eye-loved blue' –
though you know there's nothing there.

And is it no thing
that touches my heart and hurts it
and makes me want, *vow*
to be clear-coloured and utterly truthful
from now on always?

Although whenever I next see chicory
I have to confess I've forgotten as usual,
it lasts longer than most sermons do.

WHEN THE CAT COMES FOR A WALK

When the cat comes for a walk
she steps along lightly,
sniffs the air and waves her tail
and wields responsive whiskers.
Sometimes she drops behind or walks aside
to investigate vole trails
or catch an unwary blade of grass
as if to show that she can do without us.
But there comes a point when she stops short
and all her pride vanishes:
we have crossed an invisible boundary
and all beyond it is foreign and fearful.
She speaks her distress as clear as she can,
warning us, wanting us urgently
to turn back here.

My range is further than hers,
perhaps twice as far.
Then I reach the place where I too
begin to feel fear.
But I have been trained to think
my feelings are foolish,
and so I go on
across no man's land,
right into the enemy camp.

THE MAY-TREE

As if when a man was striding on an errand
of adult importance requiring a brief-case
a scruffy child should slip her hand in his
and he be obliged to accept her and protect her,
like this, today, the may came in my mind:
the responsibility.
                                    Though she's no child –
I've looked at her for eighteen years from the window
and she was already old when we came to this house.
Her hair straggles and one shoulder's
a little higher than the other,
result of the careless way she's been flail-cut.
She's fruitful – so-so. Fieldfares take their toll.
But she's had to be tough: she isn't beautiful.

She grows against the wire of the farmer's field,
a tree, definitely, having a naked
visible trunk unlike the opulent
Palmeresque bushes behind her in the pasture.
Now they, when they're in bloom, are radiant,
they can cause temporary transmutations
even in computer-friendly minds.
But she, even I her nearest sister, hadn't much
thought about till one day when two men came by
and stopped the tractor with the flail, got down
and shook her about and looked her over,
Was it worthwhile to keep an aging haw?
and I found myself running and trying not to scream
trying to discover I – who was always craven –
authority to hold their wanton hands.

Who smiled reassurance. Just trimming.
They knew at once what was the matter.
had seen women taken in this way before.
The smiles had more than a sprinkling of scorn.

You don't bring may blossom into the house!
Everyone's mother taught them that.
Don't be afraid, Mother, don't be afraid
if I bring it indoors inside my head
loving and learning the tree that is over against me:
I'm so afraid they will cut the may-tree down.

We can't carry the world, heroic, cracking:
Atlas was a man's misguided myth.
But let's carry a clod each
link arms and lift up a spring language
bud and break out and bring in better times.

IV

Muniments

Muniments

Muniments are defences. These pieces of writing are about ten of the hundred and more places in Britain alone where nuclear targets have been created.

Muniments are also documents preserved as evidence of privileges or rights. In these ten places, as elsewhere, people have added their lives to the humus of history; and the chronicles, books, essays and articles they wrote about such places and themselves were muniments in that sense. The writing of any local history tacitly asserts the rights of man and the privilege of being human. There are records, too, of the local plants and animals: they also have their muniments.

Much of what is here is written by other people; what I have done is to make gatherings of their observations, often in their own words. I want to bring home that all places are home.

Greenham Common, Upper Heyford, Lakenheath, High Wycombe, Faslane, Molesworth, Holy Loch, Ruislip, Fairford and Morwenstow, like other places in Britain and all over the globe, are places where people have lived and died alongside their fellow creatures and among the plants in mutual dependence on the earth. They speak in its defence.

I: GREENHAM COMMON, BERKSHIRE

When the earth was unsettled
I was exalted: my gravel floor held
while the rocks that made my sides
were washed away.
The valley of the shadow is as old as man
but I am older.

Then I was settled.
Bury's Bank crosses me
by which there are or were
five round dips in the grass,
the British hutments or their cattle-pens,
with a ditch and mound enclosing them
to fence outsiders out and cattle in.

My name means 'green river-valley',
referring to the land beside the Kennet.
But later I was called Red Heath
although, ironically, that name was lost.

I am there in Domesday
twenty years after the Conquest,
with land for ten ploughs
and more than a hundred acres of meadow.

People brought beehives to me in the summer
so that the bees could browse on purple heather.

I see strange sunsets.
A man named Hockin prophesied 'the downs
and this high weird common go livid
and the valleys seem like cracks in the moon,
and yourself much less than the dust...'

The earth is unsettled
and they have built a fence of fear
nine miles round on me.
Kennet and Enborne
clasp my three hundred feet.

The sunsets may grow stranger.
The radiant dust may be the last to settle.
I am green pastures and now
I am valley of the shadow.

Women watch with me continually
certain that peace is conceivable.

Know me for what I am.

'Pregnant as the history of Upper Heyford is with lessons,
I will not stay "to point the moral or adorn the tale",
but leave that to your intelligence and reason, sincerely
hoping you will apply it.'

S.W. Pearson: *History of Upper Heyford*

Tableland, sparse trees, stonebrash:
an open book.

Ash Bank's the east bound,
known too as Wattle Bank,
known too as Aves Ditch
that some say is Offa's Ditch
that bounded kingdoms.
Westward the Cher wells.

Who walked the Port Way
that runs between them
crossing the country
from York to Southampton?
Bloody Romans.

One man went to mow . . .
How long were they farming the place
and carting fodder over the ford
before that gave it its name?

Not always hey, hey nonny
and hay harvest frolics:
many died of the Black Death.
Still it was said that angels sang at dawn
when the year brought round the village Feast
in honour of Our Lady's birth.

At the Restoration New College Oxford
were Lords of the Manor and strict with timber.
To Widdow Meacocke one Tree
was granted under Warden Woodward
to mend the couples in her kill-house.
Merry the farmer *for Quietness sake*
paid James ffletcher's parish rate;
who thereupon like the servant in Scripture
peached on a poor man for stealing corn.
He kept a mastiff, blocked a footpath:
ffletcher didn't like his neighbours.
He dumped a sick cow's carcase in the spring
and fouled it: evident malice
the Warden saw at last, and sadly wrote
'hee is not indeed what hee would seem to bee'.

Tableland, sparse trees, stonebrash:
apt for landings.
The book is shut and marked Top Secret.
Kingdoms are boundless
from the air.
The Port Way is blocked
and at night the camp is lighted like a city,
a disinfected, cultureless, bland city
of a newer empire.
You cannot hear the angels, only engines.
Who gave them leave to make a kill-house?
We did? For quietness' sake?

Fletcher, my friend, I know you.
You, like the poor, are always with us.
Fighting you with laws and fists
is human life, is aboriginal.
Haul out the cow and the spring runs clean.
But this is different.

Flint axe, copper dagger, Roman brooch:
always people there between fen and breck
alongside the rabbits and plovers and curlews
scratching the sand.

Ground they broke with plough or spade
the Celts called breck; but breck goes back
and to Saxons the word meant waste,
where water is brackish and bracken grows.
Now it is land that is tilled from time to time.

Over the North Sea and up the Ouse
and up the Little Ouse to a hythe on the fen's edge,
unpromising land, Danes came and settled.
'Landing-place of Laca's people': Lakenheath.

Others make tunnels besides the rabbits.
There are tales of a passage under the fens:
they say it was there that Hereward hid.

Alan of Walsingham, Prior of Ely,
owned land there under Edward III;
and inquisitors sent to assess one ninth
of corn, lambs, wool, for fighting the French,
wrote: 'nihil solvit, nec solvere vult'.
Alan, in English, refused to pay.

This was the muster of Lakynghyve,
its civil defence in Tudor times:
princypall archers xii
able archers ii
fifteen princypall bylmen
and thirteen able.
And the store of arms was seven halberds
seven swords and seven daggers
and seven harness for three horse.

Small slidings of sand are incessant;
it moves and settles like the people.
Once the wind whipped up
a giant sandstorm like a revolution,
but they shovelled and patched and life went on.

'Nothing can be more desolate and forlorn
than the situation of Lakenheath...'
David Davy hurried away
after noting a galilee in the church.
Some find God in the wilderness;
but if some have found it godforsaken

do we still give Caesar more than his due?
Here, now, is his camp that can lay waste
the earth and all that therein is.
O the sweet cry of the ringed plover
over the breck...

What does it mean to talk about *our country?*
In Bucks it used to mean this bit of Bucks.
Batter was common for a sloping bank
and *blizzy* was a blazing fire.
The grey herb southernwood that has so many names,
lad's love, that Edward Thomas wrote about,
they knew as *kiss-i-my-corner*, wren was *tickety*,
and creeping saxifrage was *thread-of-life*.

He would have been a *bodger*,
turning the local beechwoods into chairs.
She would have got her living *at the pillow*:
bone-lace and chairs our country's noted for.

The Chiltern hills have mainly dry valleys
so Wycombe grew and took its name from water:
'valley-in-which-there-is-a-stream'.
And the hills surrounding it seemed good defences.
But neither Keep nor Castle hill availed:
a Roman pavement in a nearby field
has 'a Beast at the centre in a circle
like a dog standing sideways by a tree'.
Deliver my darling from the power of the dog
that still stands at the centre of the circle
pissing on the Tree of Life.

The Mayor and Corporation in the eighteenth century
received a distribution for defence
of muskets swords and bandoliers.
Now they get pamphlets with tall stories in.

A local poet wrote in 1848:

And here the young, oh! guard and bless!
And may they, as their days increase,
Find wisdom's ways are pleasantness,
And all her paths are paths of peace.

God guard them still in this strange century,
crouched in the mud beside their peace-camp fire.

In 1936 'on a starry night...Bomber Command was born':
glad tidings from a history of the Air Force...
What does it mean to talk about *our country*?
This land was guarded by the National Trust,
yet that raw *batter* marks a nuclear bunker.
Tickety go computerised controls:
outside, the wren is burning in the *blizzy*.
O quickly *kiss-i-my-corner* while there's time!
Parodied by the wires beneath its roots
can *thread-of-life* survive at Walter's Ash?

This is how Faslane was fashioned,
the small and beautiful bay where the burn
ran murmuring into the loch:
all these lands and lochs were the slow work of ice
and species by species after the thaw
the kingdoms began to colonise until
all along Garelochside whins and wild roses
ramped, and sloes, and there was sweeting of birds
and sweet scents from copsewood and shrubs,
and there was man.

Climb from Faslane
up the glen, over heather,
past ancient boulders left by the ice
through the peat hagg where white
pebbles glitter in the sun
and up the grassy face of Maol am Fheidh:
there's a fine peep of the loch.

Or look, doubled beauty:
moonlight on Gareloch,
stars in the water.
Still reflections...
such abundance:
why is peace so hard to grasp?

If not beauty, fear might teach it:
each croft kept its crosscuts of iron;
flesh cooled to hear the wolf's howl
beyond the circle of the firelight.
Or grief?
Fire and sword, Haco the Dane,
always 'thift, reff, and uther ennormities',
Colquoons and Macgregors,

blood in the rowan-hung waters of Fruin,
blood on the blue-grey rocks of the Glen of Sorrow,
and still a mound to mark the mass grave...
How much is enough?

John McLeod Campbell believed that love was
and he preached that love in his parish of Row
saying that Christ had saved every one.
And his people loved him and might have loved God through him.
But the Gospel of Peace is too lawless for churches and synods.
The General Assembly made him leave his kirk
though his father said he was proud of such a son
'and although his brethren cast him out
the Master whom he serves will not forsake him'.
He settled in Rosneath, across the loch,
and called his home Achnashie: Field of Peace.

Some trees grow quietly and when they're felled
show ring after ring of years you never guessed.
Molesworth's that kind of tree, rooted in clay,
a place that history hasn't noticed
except that a nineteenth-century botanist
observed an alchemilla there – a common one,
but very rare in the south and east.

The meaning of Molesworth is Mul's enclosure.
And who was Mul when he was at home?
I daresay he was a desperado:
to capture the place and then to keep it
he must have been somewhat larger than life

like St Christopher on the wall of the church
with his halo and beard and big red cloak
and the tiny Christ-child on his shoulder.

From the ancient Fayway take the long view
over the fen levels' inland islands
each with a cluster of trees and a church,
and houses, and mills once worked by the wind
that blows over the wolds, the natural wind,
and the long sweeps of the Ouse...

In Huntingdonshire to call the cows in
coof coof was what you said
tig tig would fetch the pigs in
dill dill would bring the ducks,
drive the sheep in – *heu heu* –
the only way with woolly pates...

Now we're all in Mul's enclosure.
Mul, come back and be our Noah.
Whistle for the pigeons, *whew! whew!*
...perhaps they'll tell us when it's safe...
Will there be another rainbow?
Show us a sign.

St Christopher's gums begin to bleed.

Dear Mun –

you whose havingness dwindled to this pin point:
that you felt a jealous anger when
'your' angel visited someone else,
and prayed to God to send you further affliction
(not seeing that this, precisely, was it),
specified sore bodily sickness
to make you 'worthy' of keeping him to yourself! –

look out from the door of your cell,
see how when the tide is full the breaking waves
still whiten the grass fringe of the fields with a coating of salt
as they did then.

That is Dunoon
that once was a good place to drink goat's whey
and those are the villages of the shore in a circle from south to north,
Hunters Quay, Ardnadam, Sandbank, Kilmun, Strone.
But look beyond, out in the loch.
You do not know what those are
and I am ashamed to explain.
Father, this is a small place,
but the world has grown...
there are factories where they make...
unmaking

...People everywhere assent to the sacrilege...
It is unholy. I am ashamed.

Mun, there are more men than in your day
and their sins are the same but they have learned to breed them.
I'm ashamed to admit what those things are for,
but many people know what they are for
and many are not ashamed.
They do not know that holy means healthy,
that holy means inviolable

and that they have brought their division
into a place where wholeness was sought for and found,
not in humility seeking a cure, but with pride.
We hold nothing sacred any more.

Severe even among ascetics
you whose struggle with sin was so stern
that you made this a place for fear and trembling
holy
yet still in a passion of perfection fell foul of temptation
still were a man
intercede for us,
tell how it is for our kind
that beyond all belief we are blind and still
do not know what we do
do not see how those shapes are more monstrous
than ever wallowed in a primaeval pool
or rose from the unconscious mind in myth,
do not recognise hell's brood when we see it
but proudly acknowledge these fine children ours.

Holy St Munnu, friend of Columba,
pray for us
now.

Not to go forward is to go back.
Argent on a Mount in Base Vert
a hurst of Oak trees fructed proper...
a Mitre between two Fleur de Lys...
a Boar passant Sable armed:
granted in nineteen thirty-seven
to Ruislip-Northwood Urban District Council
in the corner of Middlesex later called Little America
soon after lost in a London Borough.
Non progredi est regredi
was the motto that went with the coat of arms.

But run the film backwards and see what regression would mean:
watch Ruislip residents rapidly running away –
(you do not live in Ruislip, one resides) –
the Americans cross the Atlantic headed for home;
see how the fences and sheds are unleashing the grass,
as Sir John Betjeman trains north-west from London
to 'Where a few surviving hedges keep alive our lost Elysium',
where sooted trees and the moths that bred blackest to match them –
Waved Umber, Marbled Minor, Pale Brindled Beauty,
Green, Grey, White, Spotted and Brindled Pugs,
Spring Usher, Willow Beauty, Nut Tree Tussock –
clear and become themselves again.
The War stops at the start and Ruislip stops producing
a thousand anti-aircraft guns a month.
Now too the rail rolls back and London's at arm's length.
In the Parish of Ruislip the Reverend Roumieu
wishes 'that time with all its changes
may leave the Ruislip of the Future
the happiness of being the country village
it now is'
and built-up Eastcote's one of *Brewer's Beauties*,
'a deeply-retired and rural hamlet'.
They're skating on the River Pinn this winter –
see the candles burning on the ice!

Back in the Commonwealth savour the almost anarchic
agreement mead bitweene Nayebours
for the renewing and Mainetaining of ouer orders
of ouer feelds of Ruyslipp
which followed the weakening of the Manor Court.
On, that is, back, but always swine and cattle,
oaks and hornbeams, linking the years together;
though trees must be cut to order for making weapons
– 'springalds and other engines' –
and trees must be cleared and land ploughed
if London needed hay.
And even in Tudor times there were some enclosures:
'the people turned out and the praise of God destroyed'.

Sometimes given and sometimes snatched,
run the spool faster and the Manor passes
from hand to hand like a ball:
scholars of Cambridge had it from the Crown
who took it from Somerset, who said
'you did a most ungrateful thing to me at the end of my day...
so you take, nay rather, seize, wide and fertile estates';
but by him it was seized from the monks of Bec
(hence the Mitre and Fleur de Lys)
who were given it by Ernulf de Hesdin
who at the Conquest ousted Wluuard Wit.
Meanwhile the land itself changed less than it has this century.
Norman Sir William fitzStephen rode north-west from London
and this is what he saw:
'pasture lands and a pleasant flat space of meadow
intersected with running waters...
a great forest with wooded glades and lairs of wild beasts,
deer both red and fallow, wild boars and bulls':
Ruislip, that took its name from *rush* and *leap*,
the place where you could cross the River Pinn.

IX: FAIRFORD WINDOWS

Wealthy John Tame five hundred years ago
had this church built out of Cotswold sheep.
We cannot see it as they saw it then:
dirt and lichen dim the coloured windows,
soften the brash conviction; jumbled leads,
botched cracks, blurred lines and time have made obscure
the story of the faith in images,
'the Bible of the poor'.
                              Yet they survived;
figures on glass fragile as flesh is frail,
somehow disarming Puritan rage,
removed and hidden in 1939 from unimpassioned bombs.

Our modern weapons leave no time for that,
nor any hearts to write the story on.
Stiff-necked sightseers we go the round,
sipping the colours like wine,
trying to make out the disfigured face of God.

First light.
In the garden.
Theft of knowledge.
The green tree spoiled.
Eve and the Tempter look alike.

Second light.
Moses on holy ground.
Revelation.
Gift of knowledge.
The green tree burns uneaten...

Speaking likenesses, knowable people,
Eve in the garden, Moses, Mary,
Joseph, Pilate, Peter, Thomas,
Matthew, Mark, Isaiah, David,
Augustine, Solomon, Judas, John.
And among the rest John Tame's wife Alice
kneels trustingly close by her risen Lord;
and beyond the open tomb the River Coln
winds its familiar way through Gloucestershire.

Mediaeval art has made the Doom too tidy.
We cannot see it as they saw it then.
We have conceived a child we dare not know
– no red devils, no blue devils – mankind,
whose crawling flesh gapes at itself in terror.

We do not know whether that man was God;
but words that are not made flesh are merely idols,
peace, freedom, justice, *caritas*, truth;
and as we know that what we do
threatens his likenesses,
so we know ourselves judged
as the sun streams gold through the west window
by this one who sits upon a rainbow
with our world at his wounded feet.

On Sharton Moor in Morwenstow
both Tamar and the Torridge rise
beside the barrows of the ancient dead.
Torridge flows off eastwards into Devon
and Cornwall's Tamar makes its way down south,
marks the beginning of a new kingdom.

Here Robert Hawker, priest and ballad-maker,
wrote his *Song of the Western Men*
sitting under a stag-horned oak
in Sir Beville's Walk in Stowe Wood.
And shall Trelawny die?

'You've got birds – you've got angels:
ubi aves ibi angeli'
quoth the Parson upon a time.
He recognised a need to feel defended
and he asked God to send strong angels.
He prayed for rooks and the rooks came.
One year in Lent (always the demons' time)
he prayed a secret prayer three times a day
'Let not any Adversary despoil thine Inheritance';
'defend this thy Sanctuary from the Envy and Violence
of wicked and covetous Men'.
The Parson strewed the chancel floor with wormwood.
He strewed it with sweet marjoram and thyme.
He grew columbines, cowslips and Barnaby's thistle,
lady's smock, lilies and Timothy grass
in the church garden.

Hither Americans probably homesick
came who never heard of 'cowslips'.
John Doe chews, yawns. Oh, the chasm of that yawn!
The world could fall into it and be lost for ever.
He boogies idly to his Walkman,
when he isn't listening for the damned commies,
to shut out the sound of that goddam sea.

And it is terrible.
Come to Hawker's look-out on the cliff.
Beyond Lundy, Labrador; that's where the wind's from.
Every bush in the green combe below
leans inland.
Hearken to the tale the far-fetched waves
tell of the wide, wild Atlantic
as they lash the rocks and break
and break ships, sailors, hearts,
against the iron coast.
Modryb Marya! It's a wicked coast.

The National Trust owns Vicarage Cliff
and Hawker's look-out at Morwenstow;
but can we trust the National Trust
to remember that even Eng-land is held in trust from God?

Modryb Marya, pray for her!
(In these parts the Mother of God
is known as Aunty Mary.)
Women all are virgin to begin with
and all in time come to bear
children, or sorrows, or both;
we might do well to work in women's ways,
like Aunty Mary or like Aunt Morwenna,
whose holy spring still issues from the shale,
a silver thread of hope.

SOME SOURCES FOR *MUNIMENTS*

The Victoria History of the Counties of England
Ordnance Survey Maps
English Place-names county volumes
The Oxford English Dictionary

Transactions of the Newbury District Field Club, Vol.5, 1911
Domesday Book 5: Berkshire, ed. Philip Morgan, 1979
J.R.A. Hockin, *On Foot in Berkshire*, 1934

William King, *Annals of Heyford Warren otherwise Upper Heyford in the
    County of Oxfordshire*, 1865
S.W. Pearson, *History of Upper Heyford*, 1907
Oxfordshire Record Society, *The Progress Notes of Warden Woodward round
    the Oxfordshire Estates of New College Oxford 1659-1675*, transcribed
    and edited by R.L. Rickard, 1945

Proceedings of the Suffolk Institute of Archaeology and History
W.G. Clark, *In Breckland Wilds*, 1975

Thomas Langley, *The History and Antiquities of the Hundred of Desborough,
    and the Deanery of Wycombe, in Buckinghamshire; including the Borough
    Towns of Wycombe and Marlow*, 1797
Parker, *Early History and Antiquities of Wycombe*
L.J. Mayes, *History of the Borough of High Wycombe from 1890*
Henry Kingston, *The History of High Wycombe with Recollections of my
    native town including anecdotes, biography, oral reminiscences, poems,
    etc. etc.*, 1848
B.E. Escott, *A History of the Royal Air Force in High Wycombe*
H. Harman, *Buckinghamshire Dialect*, 1929, repr.1970

W.C. Maughan, *Annals of Garelochside*, 1896

Huntingdon Rural District Council Official Guide
C.F. Tebbutt, Articles on Huntingdonshire Folklore in *Transactions of
    the Cambridgeshire and Huntingdonshire Archaeological Society*
Howard Coote, *While I Remember*, 1937
Niklaus Pevsner, *The Buildings of England: Bedfordshire, Huntingdon and
    Peterborough*, 1968

Ordnance Gazeteer of Scotland, ed. F.H. Groome, 1894
James B. Johnston, *Place Names of Scotland*, 3rd ed. 1934, repr.1970

Nigel Tranter, *Argyll and Bute*, 1977
Butler's *Lives of the Saints*, ed. H. Thurston and D. Attwater, 1956
Maurice Lindsay, *The Lowlands of Scotland: Glasgow & the North*, 2nd
 ed. 1973

John J. Roumieu, *Ruislip, A History of the Parish and its Church*, 1875
L.E. Morris, *A History of Eastcote*, 1955, & *A History of Ruislip*, 1956
Ruislip-Northwood, The Development of an Urban District 1904-1965
Bruce Stevenson, *Middlesex*, 1972
Hillingdon Official Handbook 1973
Journal of the Ruislip & District Natural History Society
Gerald Dawe, *The Secret War*

Richard Corbet, *Upon Fairford Windows* (in Chalmers' *English Poets*)
T.D. Fosbrook, *The History of Gloucestershire*, 1807
J.G. Joyce, *The Fairford Windows*, 1972
Oscar G. Farmer, *Fairford Church and its Stained Glass Windows*

R.S. Hawker, *A Secret Prayer*, 1843
Lake's Parochial History of Cornwall, 1867, repr. J. Polsue 1974
R.S. Hawker, *Cornish Ballads*, 1869
S. Baring-Gould, *The Vicar of Morwenstow*
Derek Parker, *The West Country*, 1973
Edward C. Pyatt, *Cornwall Coast Path*, 1976